Original title:
Shoes to Walk With You

Copyright © 2025 Creative Arts Management OÜ
All rights reserved.

Author: Julian Prescott
ISBN HARDBACK: 978-1-80586-023-5
ISBN PAPERBACK: 978-1-80586-495-0

Alongside You

In mismatched colors, we stride with glee,
Your left foot's dancing, while mine's got a flea.
Two clumsy companions, a side-splitting sight,
Our soles are just itching for a wild night.

Silent Footfalls

We tiptoe past puddles, trying to glide,
But trips and stumbles make us both slide.
Each squeaky step echoes laughter so bright,
Our shadows are guffawing, what a weird sight!

Echoes of Our Steps

With every footfall, we cause quite the ruckus,
Your flip-flops are flapping, my loafers are chuckus.
The ground starts to shake with our goofy parade,
It's a symphony of giggles, a footwear charade.

Two Pairs, One Journey

In sneakers, in sandals, we march down the lane,
Dodging lost flip-flops, it's all in the game.
With laughter as fuel, on this path we run,
Two pairs side by side, making mischief, what fun!

Two Pairs, One Road

Two pairs of soles, with laughter to share,
Side by side wandering without a care.
One chases sunshine, the other a snail,
Together we giggle wherever we sail.

SwappingOur shoes, what a sight to behold,
Two left feet, but our hearts are bold.
Tripping on laces, we tumble and roll,
Yet our friendship keeps warming the stroll.

Strides in Sync

Our strides align like a quirky dance,
Invisible sync, oh what a chance!
Tripping on cobblestones, laughing so loud,
With every misstep, we draw in a crowd.

One hops, one skips, it's a circus act,
Mixing our rhythm, that's just a fact.
But when we tumble, all joy is found,
In clumsy chaos, our love's so profound.

Walking in Your Footprints

I follow the tracks, they zigzag and weave,
In mismatched styles, I choose to believe.
With goofy strides, we carve our own path,
Turning the sidewalk to a stage of our laugh.

Wherever you wander, I bumble along,
In footprints so silly, we both sing a song.
Right next to you, I'll stumble and trip,
Each moment together, a quirk on this trip.

Trails of Friendship

On this trail, we waddle and glide,
Both cracking up with each silly slide.
Stomp in a puddle, send water in flight,
Oh, the memories we make, what a delight!

Side by side through mud and through muck,
In every adventure, we're just out of luck.
Yet laughter's our compass, guiding us true,
In this fun-filled journey, I'll follow with you.

Pathways Worn Together

Two mismatched pairs, oh what a sight,
Stumbling down lanes, laughter takes flight.
One's too big, the other's too small,
Yet together we conquer, we laugh through it all.

Pavement dances, as we hop and skip,
Side by side on this wild road trip.
With quirky steps and no perfect plan,
We make every moment, just because we can.

Soles of Companionship

In a cupboard they linger, gathering dust,
Yet on our feet, it's a must!
Bright polka dots, and stripes with flair,
Who knew silly socks could take us anywhere?

With each clumsy step, we share the giggles,
As puddles splash, and the earth wiggles.
Through muddy paths and grassy glades,
Our quirky soles leave colorful shades.

Steps by Your Side

A tap, a twirl, and a surprised leap,
Who thought our feet could make such a peep?
We bob and weave, like a wobbly dance,
Each misstep giving the next chance.

Your left foot's ahead, while mine takes a right,
We shuffle, we stumble, bring on the delight!
No straight lines here, it's a zigzag race,
Just two happy souls, keeping up the pace.

The Journey Beneath Our Feet

From sandy dunes to bustling streets,
Our soles are sidekicks on wild retreats.
They squeak and squish, with every stride,
Creating a symphony of joy inside.

We leap over cracks, avoid doggy surprise,
Our cautious advance, oh how time flies!
The world beneath is a vibrant hum,
As we skip along, our hearts thrum.

Side by Side in Motion

Two pairs of feet, a dance in sight,
Shimmy and shake, what a funny sight!
We stumble and trip, but oh what glee,
Laughing so hard, it's just you and me.

Puddle jumps turn to splashes wide,
Like two clumsy ducks, we glide and slide.
With each step taken, we giggle more,
Each misstep brings a hearty roar!

Weaving Footprints Together

In the sand, our marks are a silly mess,
Like a drunken crab, we guess and guess!
Twisting and turning on this winding track,
Our laughter echoes, there's no looking back.

A hop, skip, and a jump, then we fall,
Land in a heap, and we can't stand tall.
With footprints tangled in every way,
We're partners in fun, come what may!

The Rhythm of Together

Step to the left, then shuffle to the right,
Two left feet, but we still feel light.
A tap dance started turns into a race,
With giggles that travel from place to place.

Our feet move fast, like a wild parade,
Twisting and turning, not a charade.
Oh what a sight, a comical spree,
Two silly partners in perfect harmony!

Guided by Each Other's Steps

Hand in hand, we wander this lane,
Foot in a puddle, oh what a gain!
We swap our moves, I step on your toes,
A comedy act, that's how it goes!

With a wink and a nudge, we float like a breeze,
Twisty turns that bring us to our knees.
In this big world, we dance with a cheer,
Two goofy pals with nothing to fear!

Companions on the Way

In mismatched laces we set out today,
With one left foot so far astray.
Together we giggle, stumble, and sway,
As two goofballs make their clumsy display.

With a squeaky step and a wobbly glide,
Who knew our journey would turn into a ride?
We trip on laughter, no need to hide,
As we march through life, side by side.

Steps Alongside You

Oh look at us, a sight quite absurd,
Your toes are cramped, my ankles blurred.
We'll dance through puddles, haven't you heard?
With goofy grins and hopes unstirred.

We'll take it slow, there's no need to rush,
Each small adventure, pure joy, like a hush.
Watch out for mud, it's a slippery crush,
But hand-in-hand, we'll always feel plush.

Soles of Togetherness

With heels that squeal and toes that shout,
Our paths ring loud, we're in and out.
You tease my step, I twist about,
In folly and fun, we conquer doubt.

As shadows dance like a playful tease,
Our soles will wiggle, shake with ease.
In this crazy world, let's take a breeze,
With chuckles wafting like falling leaves.

Pathways We Share

Two pairs of soles on a road so wide,
Your left shoe's spry, mine glides with pride.
Together we wander, what a wild ride,
As we chase the sun and the jokes you've supplied.

In mismatched colors, our journey unfolds,
With each little stumble, a story retold.
Through laughter and mishaps, the world feels bold,
As we track the path, forever gold.

Footsteps in Time

Tiny boots, they stomp and squeak,
Marching on, though feeling weak.
With each step, a chuckle grows,
Waddling 'round, where no one goes.

Laces tangled, what a mess,
Tried to dance, but lost the dress.
Bouncing here, and tripping there,
Who knew walking's such a dare?

Socks that clash, a fashion feast,
Two left feet, I'm not deceased!
With goofy strides, I claim the floor,
My quirky path, forever more.

Every step, a tale to tell,
No rhythm found, but all is swell.
In silly shoes, we laugh and play,
Each stumble brightens up the day.

Harmony in Motion

A pair of clogs that squeak and slide,
A ballet dancer's joy and pride.
One shoe's lost, a chase ensues,
While giggles burst, like morning dew.

Flip-flops flapping, running wild,
Barefoot toddler, nature's child.
With every trot, a goofy spin,
It's hard to hold, the laughter in.

High-tops bouncing, what a sight,
Twisting, turning, pure delight.
My sandals sing, a jolly tune,
As we dance beneath the moon.

Four left feet, they find their groove,
Banana peels, a funny move.
In mismatched steps, we sing and sway,
Together trotting, come what may.

Strolling Through Life

In rubber boots and sandals wide,
We laugh and dance, a joyful stride.
With every step a squeak or squeal,
We stride along with zest and zeal.

On cobblestones our feet align,
Each clack and clatter, pure design.
A shuffle here, a slide, a spin,
With every turn, we break the din.

Through puddles deep and mud so thick,
We jump and splash, just for a trick.
The sun may shine, or rain may fall,
Together we just laugh through all.

In mismatched socks, we prance around,
Each wobbly step, a merry sound.
With every twist and every turn,
A lesson learned, a page to turn.

Two by Two on the Path

Two little ducks and goofy bears,
We sidestep puddles, climb the stairs.
With tangled laces tied up tight,
We bounce and giggle, what a sight!

Chasing shadows in the breeze,
Dodging raindrops with such ease.
In double steps, we twist and twirl,
Our laughter's loud, it starts to whirl.

We hop a log, then leap a stone,
Each bouncy step, we're not alone.
In sync we move, like birds in flight,
Bounding forth from morn till night.

With silly hats and trusty packs,
We dance our way along the tracks.
On this path, we're bond and glee,
Two by two, just you and me.

Bonds Beyond Boundaries

Through winding streets and grassy lanes,
With every footfall, joy remains.
In shoes of colors, bright and bold,
We forge a bond that's yet untold.

Our soles may scuff and treads may tear,
But who's to care? Fun's everywhere!
With every leap across the gap,
We'll have a laugh, or take a nap.

Through bumps and skips, we find our way,
With sunny smiles to light the day.
In silly steps, we skip and glide,
With you beside, it's all a ride.

Though paths may twist and choices bend,
I know for sure, you're my best friend.
So let us wander, stroll with cheer,
In every step, our cares disappear.

Our Journey in Motion

With shoes that squeak and one that flops,
We bounce along like little pops.
Each step a giggle, rhythm divine,
In this crazy dance, you're always mine.

We trip on cracks, but never fall,
Our laughter echoes, it fills the hall.
With every skip, our spirits soar,
Each playful step makes us want more.

In slippery slides and jumps so high,
We chase our dreams, you and I.
With a wiggle and a wiggle dance,
Life is silly, let's take a chance.

Through forests deep or city lights,
Our playful hearts bring endless sights.
So come along, let's just be free,
In this wild ride, it's you and me!

Navigating Life in Tandem

Two left feet find their groove,
Pacing through life, we quickly move.
Trip on laughter, dance on dreams,
In mismatched kicks, we're a team!

Tick-tock, we're late, oh what a race,
Stumbling 'round like we own this place.
With every step, a joyful shout,
Life's a dance, there's never a doubt!

Side by side, in colorful flair,
Wobbling friends, we have not a care.
In our travel gear, we laugh and cheer,
Every misstep, brings you near!

With each twist and turn, it's a comic scene,
Wearing bright styles, we're a funky machine.
Keep those giggles as our guide,
In this bumpy ride, you're by my side.

Heartfelt Heel-to-Toe

With clashing colors, a wondrous sight,
We stride along, in day or night.
One foot's a clown, the other a champ,
Together we sparkle, a shining lamp!

On cobblestones, we dance with flair,
Stumbling often, but we don't care.
Each step's a joke, a silly jest,
In this trotting life, we're truly blessed!

Twirling wildly, watch us go!
With a hop and a skip, we put on a show.
Our quirky steps create a rhythm,
An offbeat song, our shared schism!

From puddles splashing to hills so steep,
In this journey, our laughter we keep.
Heel-to-toe, we jive and sway,
In our silly shoes, we seize the day!

Together We Traverse

Two pairs dancing in perfect sync,
Navigating pathways, an odd link.
In one bright red and one dull blue,
We stomp ahead—who knew we'd stew?

Slipping on joy, we laugh out loud,
Our two-left-feet bring a merry crowd.
Backwards striding, oh what a sight,
Life's a circus; we're taking flight!

Wobbling forward, we trip on glee,
Each misstep, a new melody.
Side by side, we twirl and spin,
The fun we have is always a win!

Through puddles we splash, with giggles galore,
In this silly stroll, we aim to explore.
Together we traverse, hand-in-hand,
In our own rhythm, we perfectly stand.

Harmonized Beats

United steps on this fun-filled spree,
Matching strides, just like TV.
You hop and skip, while I prance,
Our silly moves, the best romance!

With mismatched laces, we take our cue,
Who knew this trot would feel so new?
Laughing at stumbles, we keep it bright,
In our groovy lanes, we own the night.

Pitter patter, we just can't wait,
In tangled threads, we seal our fate.
Every step's a song, in laughs we trust,
Together we groove; it's a must!

So here's to the fun, as we make our play,
In perfect harmony, we sway away.
A dance of two, with tales to tell,
In this laughter-filled ride, all is well!

A Walk Beside You

Two left feet on a stroll,
Trip over grass, that's our goal.
Side by side, we laugh and sway,
Who knew walking could be this way?

Pacing slow like a turtle friend,
Step by step, around the bend.
With each giggle, the miles fly,
Together, we'll learn to glide—oh my!

Journeys in Tandem

With mismatched socks, we hit the street,
Dodging puddles, oh what a feat!
Stumbling forth, it's quite a dance,
In this journey, there's room for chance.

You step left, I step right,
Chasing shadows in the light.
Every shuffle sparks a grin,
In tandem, we're destined to win!

Sandals of Companionship

In flip-flops that squeak and slide,
One falls down while one will glide.
A comedic pair on summer's path,
With each footfall, we stir up laughter's bath.

With toes exposed to the sunny cheer,
We giggle loud; we have no fear.
Side by side, we leap and lurch,
In these sandals, we go—let's search!

Steps in Harmony

One foot forward, then the next,
You trip, I laugh—oh, what a text!
Like a rhythm in a silly song,
Who knew stepping could feel so wrong?

Each clumsy twirl brings a new delight,
Together we dance, such a funny sight.
With every laugh, we write a tune,
In our steps, we twinkle like a boon!

Pathways of Connection

In a world of busy feet,
With strides that can't be beat,
We trip and sometimes fall,
Yet we laugh through it all.

Side by side we wander,
Our giggles growing fonder,
With every step we take,
A silly dance we make.

We've got a flair for moves,
Like jazz hands in grooves,
And when our paths align,
It's a dash of pure divine.

Together we will roam,
Creating our own home,
Each footfall tells a tale,
Like ducks upon a trail.

A Shared Walk

Let's stroll down sidewalk lanes,
In mismatched silly chains,
With squeaky soles that squeak,
And laughter that's unique.

We'll step on puddles bright,
Splash around with pure delight,
As ducks give us a stare,
While we dance without a care.

Each twist and little turn,
Brings giggles that we'll earn,
With every little hop,
Our humor will not stop!

So come on, take my hand,
Let's jiggle through this land,
With a clumsy bounce, we'll see,
How silly fun can be!

Motions of Mutuality

In step with goofy grins,
We twirl and jump like twins,
Wobbling just a bit,
Who knew this walk was lit?

With a rhythm all our own,
We've got a silly tone,
Swaying left and right,
We laugh 'til late at night.

Every footfall makes a sound,
Like clowns upon the ground,
We orchestrate our fun,
Our adventure's just begun!

With our feet in sync, we giggle,
As the world starts to wiggle,
This mismatch will ignite,
A journey filled with light.

Stitched Soles

With every step we take,
Our soles begin to shake,
Funny sounds erupt,
Our joy can't be disrupted.

We hop on fluffy clouds,
Laughing with the crowds,
Our mismatched laces swirl,
As we dance, twirl, and whirl.

With quirky, playful threads,
We weave what's in our heads,
Each loop a silly shout,
That echoes all about.

Our soles may not be neat,
But they carry laughter's beat,
In every flop and turn,
There's a lesson here to learn.

Stitched Hearts

Two soles paired up for fun,
Hand in hand, we run,
A patchwork of delight,
Our hearts as light as night.

As we step in silly sync,
We find time to rethink,
Each chuckle at mistakes,
Is a joy that never shakes.

In mismatched colors bright,
We'll dance until the night,
With laughter stitched in seams,
We'll weave a life of dreams.

So here's to every stride,
With you right by my side,
In laughter, we connect,
A perfect chance to reflect.

Friendship on the Ground

Two left feet and one big clown,
Stumbling through the sleepy town.
With every step, we laugh and cheer,
Who needs a map? We're pioneers!

Laces tied in quite a knot,
Dancing through the parking lot.
Every misstep's a joyful sound,
In this dance, our chaos found.

Together, We Roam

One tiny shoe, one giant flip,
Plodding down this wacky trip.
With mismatched styles, we strut around,
Making giggles the only sound.

Through puddles and mud, we take our chance,
The world's our stage for a silly dance.
With each tumble, our spirits lift,
Friendship's the greatest, goofball gift.

The Joinery of Journeys

Bouncing here and bouncing there,
Worn-out soles, no sign of care.
With every step, our stories blend,
Who knew mischief could be so grand?

One sock on left, and none for right,
We venture forth with sheer delight.
In this parade of quirks and charms,
Let's wander where adventure warms.

Walks that Unite

With duck-shaped shoes and squeaky heels,
Our journey's fun, that's how it feels.
Two pals with zest, a clumsy crew,
Stomping through life, oh what a view!

Funky kicks and matching grace,
Laughter echoes as we race.
Every road seems like a play,
Together, we shine in our own way.

Footpaths of Love

On our path, we trip and slide,
Laughter echoes, can't help but bide.
With each step, a little dance,
We stumble forward, take a chance.

In mismatched styles, we embrace,
Tangled laces, a funny chase.
With goofy grins, we walk the line,
A twist of fate, our hearts align.

The mud, it splatters, oh what fun,
Each little laugh, we both have won.
In puddles deep, we leap and shout,
Together, love blooms, no doubt!

With each misstep, a brand new plot,
In comedy, we take our shot.
Each pathway leads to new surprise,
In this odd dance, love never dies.

Close Quarters of Shadows

In tight corners, we find our way,
Fumbling close, with much to say.
Our shadows twist, they laugh and tease,
As we stumble in perfect ease.

With each misstep, we crack a grin,
In this close dance, we'll always win.
Bumping elbows, what a delight,
In fun-filled chaos, hearts feel light.

When shadows stretch, we play and run,
Each little fall brings so much fun.
In the night, we chase and twirl,
Together we create a whirl.

Navigating love, it's quite the feat,
In these close quarters, our hearts meet.
Beneath the stars, we find our groove,
In laughter, we both find our move.

Unity in Each Step

With every step, a comic tale,
A wobbly stride, we will not fail.
In perfect sync, we laugh and play,
Uniting joy in each ballet.

As feet collide, we squeak and slide,
Building memories, side by side.
In silly skips, our hearts will race,
In this grand dance, we find our place.

With playful jests, we trip and cheer,
Each little stumble draws you near.
In joyous fits, we take the road,
Our steps unite, lighten the load.

In clumsy rhythm, we discover bliss,
Each joyful fall, a cherished kiss.
With every twist, our love is blessed,
In unity, we find our rest.

Together, We Wander

In wandering shoes, we roam afar,
With goofy moves, we chase the stars.
Each twist and turn, a new surprise,
Together we venture, fun in our eyes.

With every step, a silly grin,
A dance of joy, let the games begin.
We leap and laugh, through rain or shine,
In shared adventures, our hearts entwine.

Between outbursts, we twirl and fall,
With every giggle, we heed the call.
Through winding paths, our spirits soar,
In this wild journey, who could want more?

As laughter rings and moments blend,
We wander on, hand in hand, my friend.
In each stride, our story spins,
Together we wander, where fun begins.

The Connection Beneath

Two mismatched socks, they dance away,
One wants to waltz, the other to sway.
Together they scamper, in quiet delight,
Laughing at puddles, with all of their might.

Stomping through mud with a squeaking sound,
A pair of old shoes, together they're bound.
They trip over laces and slip on the grass,
But oh what a joy, as they tumble and pass.

In the realm of the soles, it's quite a scene,
Life's goofy stroll, like a lively routine.
With sunshine and giggles, they skip through the day,
Glancing at clouds, come what may!

Sharing these paths, what a curious fate,
Two travelers dancing at a delightful rate.
With every squishy step, they'll cheekily roam,
Wherever they wander, they'll always feel home.

A Journey Hand in Hand

Left and right, they strut so bold,
Two delightful companions, never too old.
They stroll past the shops, laughing with glee,
And trip over cracks, just wait and see!

One says, 'I'm tired,' the other replies,
'Let's take a break, beneath those blue skies.'
They plop on a bench, and a seagull will stare,
As crumbs from their snack float into the air.

With laces entwined, they giggle and grin,
Each step an adventure, let the fun begin!
They'll hop over puddles, chase shadows with flair,
And trip on each joke hanging in the air.

So here's to the stroll, as silly as pie,
With a misshaped adventure that never runs dry.
Step by step, hand in hand, they will play,
In this joyous journey, come laugh come what may!

Tandem Trails

A flip-flop and high heel, what a sight!
They wander the streets in sheer delight.
One's always glamorous, one's comfy and fun,
Together they shine like the evening sun.

They sneek past the puddles with playful intent,
One giggles, 'Let's leap!' while the other is bent.
A tumble, a stumble, and off go the shades,
As they snicker and chuckle at their funny escapades.

In a race down the block, they might trip on a cat,
But laughter erupts, oh imagine that!
Two soles on an adventure, eclectic and bright,
With the quirkiest steps, they twirl through the night.

So on with the journey, the zany parade,
Through parks, over bridges, new trails to invade.
With every odd pair, a partnership true,
Wandering together, just us two!

The Shared Adventure

With every clomp and every clang,
They dance through the streets, oh what a bang!
One squeaks with laughter, the other just glides,
Together they take the most playful strides.

Through rain or shine, they don't mind a bit,
One jumps so high, the other will split!
They pirouette past, causing heads to turn,
As their joyous rhythm makes the world yearn.

A tumble, a roll, what a comical scene,
As they spin down the road, a mighty machine!
With mischief in every little step they take,
They share a bond that no storm can shake.

So let's join the fun, this whimsical spree,
Two characters joined, just you and me.
In every misstep, in every little sway,
We find our adventures, come what may!

Footprints in Unity

Tiny prints in the sand,\
Side by side, we stand,\
Wobbly steps and giggles loud,\
We trip, we fall, but feel so proud.\
\
With mismatched pairs, we strut along,\
Our silly dance, a bouncy song,\
The world is big, our laughter bright,\
We fumble through the day and night.\
\
Those little marks, a story told,\
In every slip, there's joy to behold,\
A trail of fun, where this life leads,\
Together we laugh, fulfilling our needs.\
\
From puddles splashed to grassy thrills,\
Our journey's full of quirky spills,\
Each step a chance to make a friend,\
With every footprint, laughter won't end.

The Journey of Two

Two left feet on a dance floor,\
Stumbling like we've never done before,\
With every misstep, a chuckle shared,\
Who knew tripping could feel so prepared?\
\
In a race for snacks, we run like the wind,\
Only to tumble with our willy-nilly spin,\
But every awkward moment's worth a cheer,\
For in this chaos, you stay so near.\
\
From hopscotch games to leapfrog leaps,\
We find belly laughs in silly heaps,\
Navigating life with a twist and twirl,\
Two goofy souls ready to whirl.\
\
So let's decree that offbeat fun\
Is the secret spice to become one,\
A journey of two with laughter's glue,\
Where every step feels fresh and new.

Laces of Connection

Tangled laces on the floor,\
A knot of giggles, who could ask for more?\
We trip on ties, bounce back like springs,\
Life's little messes can give us wings.\
\
A race in circles, who's keeping score?\
Our mixed-up pairs are worth an encore,\
With every bumble, our bond's secure,\
A stretchy friendship, that's for sure!\
\
We dance through puddles, hearts collide,\
In a festival of fun, there's no need to hide,\
Each stumble brings priceless memories,\
Wandering together, we do what we please.\
\
So here's to laces, bright and round,\
With silly dances, our joy's unbound,\
In every twist, we find a way,\
To celebrate the lighter day.

Strolls Through Our Dreams

Taking strolls in pajamas bright,\
In our wild worlds, we take flight,\
With candy clouds and jellybean streams,\
Life takes shape from all our dreams.\
\
Through fields of giggles, we wander far,\
Finding laughter like a shooting star,\
With every skip, our spirits rise,\
Drawing happiness from the skies.\
\
In silly shoes, we bounce with glee,\
Bound by laughter, you and me,\
Silly symbols in the night,\
Dancing shadows, pure delight.\
\
As dawn approaches, we wave goodbye,\
To starry paths in our minds that fly,\
Yet in the morn, we'll find our way,\
To journey together, come what may.

Grounded in Togetherness

In a pair that's oh so grand,
We stumble, yet we take a stand.
One's too big, the other's tight,
But together, we feel just right.

A mismatch here, a color clash,
We waddle, giggle, then we dash.
In this dance, our joy will bloom,
Two left feet in one small room.

Side by side, we make a scene,
With rubber ducks and jelly beans.
Hopscotch dreams and puddle splashes,
Our quirky steps turn heads in flashes.

Through ups and downs, we laugh anew,
In bouncy soles, just me and you.
With every trip and every fall,
Our goofy sync is best of all.

Harmony of Heels

Whispers echo in the air,
As our antics play without a care.
You wear platforms, I got flats,
Together we dance, like silly cats.

You strut tall, I'm a wobbly boat,
On rocky roads, we float and gloat.
In the rhythm of our clownish sway,
We trip and giggle on our way.

With every step, our laughter rings,
Hopping like bunnies, flapping wings.
The world may shake, we just play on,
In harmony, from dusk till dawn.

So here's to moments, offbeat and bright,
In mismatched styles, we shine our light.
With clumsy grace, we dare to roam,
In this wild spree, we both feel home.

Footprints in the Sand

At the shore, we both leave traces,
As clumsy feet make silly faces.
One's a flip-flop, the other a boot,
We stomp through waves, oh what a hoot!

With sandy toes and tangled hair,
We chase the gulls as they take air.
Our footprints mix, a laughing mess,
In this wacky dance, we feel so blessed.

Who knew that sun and waves would call,
To make our laughter sail and sprawl?
In slippery antics, we twirl around,
Crashing together, laughter unbound.

As sunset glows, we grin and plot,
More silly games on this sandy lot.
With memories made beneath the sun,
In this backdrop, our joy's just begun.

The Dance of Pairing

Two odd socks on a wild spree,
Bouncing around, just you and me.
With each misstep, the laughter flows,
In this dance, our fun just grows.

The left foot leads, while the right plays coy,
Doing the tango, oh what a joy!
We spin and twirl like a circus show,
Tripping on giggles, stealing the glow.

With every stomp, the ground will shake,
Our comic rhythm, a merry quake.
In a whirl of laughter, we lose the beat,
But together, oh, it's really sweet!

So let's take flight in this silly dance,
In our funky pairs, let's take a chance.
With mismatched flair and goofy grins,
Each step we take, our fun begins!

The Voyage of Togetherness

On this grand trip, let's share a pair,
Two left feet, but who would care?
With every step, we clack and slide,
Together we giggle, no need to hide.

Stumbling through puddles, oh what a sight,
We dance in circles, what pure delight!
You lead the way, but I'm on your tail,
In this silly walk, we can't fail.

With mismatched styles, our laughter rings,
A mix of fashion, just laugh at the flings!
Through swamps and puddles our journey's fun,
Side by side, we've already won!

So let's keep walking, tripping in glee,
In this wild ride, just you and me!
No map in hand, we'll find our way,
With joy and laughter, come what may.

Sensations of Companionable Trades

I'll trade you my left for your right,
As we wander on, what a sight!
You laugh as I trip over my lace,
We tumble and giggle all over the place.

I'll barter my blisters for some of your flair,
You provide the rhythm, I'll bring the air!
With each little swap, our spirits soar,
In this fun exchange, who could want more?

From wobbly flip-flops to boots with flair,
Our mismatched gait leaves folks in despair!
Yet with each shuffle, we break out in song,
A tune of togetherness, forever strong.

So let's keep trading, as we prance and sway,
With shared laughter, let's pave our way!
In this joyful trade, let's rule the day,
Two oddballs together, come what may.

In Step With You

In your shadow, I find my beat,
A two-step shuffle, what a treat!
As we bounce along, side by side,
In this wacky world, it's a fun ride!

Popping and skipping, what's that move?
With every giggle, we find our groove!
You step on my foot, I laugh and shout,
With joy and mischief, that's what it's about!

Our toes may tangle, but who's to care?
With every misstep, we blaze our flair!
In this crazy dance, let's twirl and spin,
With you by my side, that's where I begin.

So let's keep moving, just follow the sound,
In every misstep, true joy is found!
Through clumsy laughter, we'll light the way,
Together forever, come dance and play!

Footprints in Time

With every step, we leave our mark,
A comical dance in the park!
Puddles splashed, our footprints wild,
In this journey, we're each a child.

From clumsy hops to a sideways slide,
Our goofy steps full of pride!
You trip on a stone, but laugh it off,
In this joyful journey, we can't scoff!

Through all the twists and every turn,
With love and laughter, we brightly burn!
So let's trace memories in the sand,
Together, my friend, it's simply grand.

On this path of joy, let's leave our sign,
A tapestry woven, so beautifully entwined!
As we march through life, let's make it our rhyme,
In the footprints of laughter, we'll conquer time.

Links Beneath

On sunny days, our feet collide,
With mismatched sandals, oh what a ride!
Clashing colors, a wild ballet,
As we laugh and trip on our way.

A left foot's laughing at the right,
Dancing together, what a sight!
Tangled laces bring on the fun,
Who knew that walking could weigh a ton?

Strutting proud down the crowded street,
Each step's a giggle, we can't be beat.
In this parade of silly glee,
Our journeys forge a comical spree.

At the day's end, we'll reminisce,
Over poorly tied knots and goofy bliss.
With a wink, we'll promise anew,
To keep strolling in mismatched view.

Unified Adventures

No need for GPS on this fun ride,
With clunky boots, we'll take it in stride.
You bring your left, I'll bring my right,
Together we'll cause quite the sight.

Through puddles we leap with sunny delight,
Hopping like frogs, shoes not tight.
A squishy surprise, oh what a splash,
Just two clowns making a dash!

The world's our stage, we twirl and we whirl,
Dodging the ditches, giving a twirl.
Laughing so hard, we're turning red,
And who knew socks could go on our head?

With each step, we've made memories vast,
In mismatched styles, we'll have a blast.
As we roam these curious lands,
Let's conquer the world hand in hand.

Strolls of Solidarity

Shoes of all sizes, scattered about,
We venture forth, singing and shout.
Flippers and crocs, don't care for a scheme,
Who knew our fashion was part of the dream?

Together we frolic, outside of the box,
Hopping and skipping, with flip-flop knocks.
A little misstep sends us off track,
But laughter's the fuel that brings us back!

Through ticklish grass, our toes explore,
With each funny fall, we giggle for sure.
Socks on our hands, just adds to the fun,
In the end, we'll say, that's how it's done!

Let's model our quirks for all to embrace,
In this quirky show, we've found our place.
As night falls, we'll dance under the moon,
With each silly step, we're in perfect tune.

Footpaths Entwined

Across the park, we make our way,
With a wobbly stride that steals the day.
Mismatched pairs, oh what a sight,
Two jesters prancing, bold and bright.

Tangled and twisted like a ball of yarn,
Cheeky grins making the world feel warm.
Footloose and fancy, we take a leap,
With giggles echoing, our joy runs deep.

Rounding a corner, we spot a puddle,
With a hop and a splash, we enter the muddle.
Laughing like kids, rolling on grass,
No moment wasted, oh, what a pass!

Finally, at dusk, we ponder our shoes,
The journeys we've had and a million views.
With a nod and a grin, we raise a cheer,
For the joy of the stroll with my favorite dear.

Heartbeats in Motion

In mismatched pairs, we set the scene,
With soles so odd, but hearts so keen.
We shuffle and slide, a clumsy dance,
Tripping on air, oh what a chance!

Laces untied, we laugh and fall,
Stumbling together, we rise tall.
With every step, a chuckle shared,
In wacky footsteps, this love declared!

Though blisters form and toes may ache,
Each little folly, a precious memento we make.
Wobbling forward, like penguins we glide,
In this joyful journey, you're my guide!

So let's tread lightly, with giggles and glee,
As we dance through life, just you and me.
With hearts like drums, and laughter so bright,
Our silly saunter brings pure delight!

Navigating Life's Path

With socks that clash in colors so bold,
We wander together, more stories unfold.
Through puddles and mud, we stomp with grace,
Who knew a walk could be such a race?

Our mystery map is a carnival style,
Every wrong turn lands us a smile.
We trip on the gravel, roll on the grass,
In this wobbly venture, we find love's sass!

Navigating the world, sometimes we miss,
But hold on tight—oh, what bliss!
Embracing each blunder, in coiled delight,
This goofy adventure feels perfectly right!

With quirkily linked arms, we shimmy and sway,
Bouncing through life in our own funny way.
Each step may be silly, yet gold like a ray,
Playing our part in this dance and this play!

Footsteps in Unison

Our step count rises, in sync we trot,
Each footfall's a giggle, like it or not.
Sliding on sidewalks, a mini parade,
With jigs and jumps, our faux pas displayed!

In perfect rhythm, we sway and we spin,
With two left feet, how could we win?
But laughter erupts with every misstep,
This chaotic waltz is our cheerful rep!

As rain starts to pour, we look like a sight,
Sloshing through puddles, oh what a delight!
We wade through the splashes, embracing the fun,
In puddles and giggles, our hearts weigh a ton!

A dance of mischief on this crazy route,
In a world of strange paths, we twist and we shout.
Each awkward falter is music to hear,
In these silly strides, our love comes clear!

Love's Pathway

In footwear ideal, we bravely embark,
With sandals and flops, we leave a mark.
Squeaky and squeal-y, we wobble in sync,
As giggles erupt, we're sure to not think!

Through forest trails, or city blocks,
Our mismatched journey plays tricks on clocks.
With each silly hop, and leap like a frog,
We twirl through the sunshine, and laugh through the fog!

With each sassy strut, our feet make a song,
In these joyful jaunts, nowhere feels wrong.
Hand in hand, let's skip down this lane,
With laughter our guide, we dance in the rain!

So lace up your heart, and let's feel the beat,
In this merry parade, we're light on our feet.
With laughter as treasure, let's skip and sway,
Creating our path, in the silliest way!

The Rhythm of Our Walk

We bob and weave like dancers in a line,
With one step forward, we're stepping on a dime.
You trip on air, I laugh out loud,
Together we're a quirky, happy crowd.

Your left foot's ready, my right foot is slow,
We're like a show where the actors don't know.
We twist and turn, make silly faces,
While strangers stare at our funny paces.

You say, "Watch out!" as I bump a tree,
And suddenly the world is just you and me.
The rhythm of our steps is a wobbly dance,
With every misstep, we find a new chance.

So here we go, in this delightful spree,
Whirling in laughter, just you and me.
With giggles and stumbles, we create our own groove,
In the joy of our walk, we naturally move.

Side by Side

You're on my left and I'm on your right,
Swinging our arms like we're in a fight.
A two-headed monster, we stroll down the lane,
With our silly antics, we'll never be plain.

You step in a puddle; I laugh till I die,
Splashing the water like I'm aiming high.
We're dodging each raindrop, it's an obstacle course,
With every new splash, we feel the force.

Our giggles echo as we bump into folks,
Creating a symphony of playful jokes.
You trip on your laces, I'm losing my breath,
This fun walking spree feels like a dance with death.

But what's life without laughter? So close yet so far,
We trip through the moments, like a bright shooting star.
From sidewalk to park, wherever we roam,
Being side by side, we feel so much at home.

Strides of Affection

We stride together like two clumsy deer,
With every misstep, our laughter draws near.
You say, "I'm graceful!" as you trip on a stone,
While I'm busy daydreaming and checking my phone.

Our feet are colliding, it's a comical sight,
Tangled like noodles in a pasta delight.
You challenge my speed, I pretend to be fast,
Then stumble and roll when I try to outlast.

We swing our arms, making big goofy moves,
With every little slip, our humor improves.
Each chuckle and giggle becomes a sweet blend,
In this crazy parade, I can't help but grin.

Who knew that our steps could be so much fun?
With each silly fall, we've already won.
As we roam free, our hearts start to cheer,
In these strides of affection, love's crystal clear.

In Each Other's Footsteps

We take off together, a duo on the run,
In each other's footsteps, life's never done.
I step on your heel, you step on my toe,
It tickles and giggles—oh, how we glow!

Through squishy grass and muddy patches we roam,
With a hop, skip, jump—we've made it our home.
You say, "Race you!" and off you go whizzing,
I trip on my laces—oh, how we're fizzing!

We share our secrets while sharing our stride,
With every little stumble, I'm bursting with pride.
Your laughter's contagious, it brightens the day,
In each other's footsteps, we'll find our own way.

Let's keep walking together, just me and you,
Through slips and slides, we'll always be true.
With joy in our hearts, we'll never lose track,
For in each other's footsteps, there's no looking back.

Echoes of Our Steps

When we stroll down the lane, it's a dance,
Our feet tap a tune, oh what a chance.
With each clumsy stomp, laughter fills the air,
Like two marching bands, we make quite a pair.

The left goes left, the right goes right,
Oh, the chaos we bring, oh what a sight!
Side-stepping puddles, what a splashy show,
Each step a giggle, where else would we go?

With rhythm so wild, we spin around,
Wobbling like jelly, both feet off the ground.
Bumps and giggles, a bumpity bump,
In our silly dance, we both take a jump.

In our flight of fancy, we lose all our grace,
Tripping on laughter, we fall on our face.
Echoes of our steps will bounce off the walls,
With joy in our hearts, we'll answer the calls.

A Path We Create

On the sidewalk of life, we skip and we trot,
Inventing our rules, in the silly spot.
With each vibrant print, we doodle the way,
Making up paths, like a daring ballet.

You step on my heel, I spin in a whirl,
Our quirky partnership makes my head twirl.
The ground giggles beneath as we take flight,
Every misstep just feels so delightfully right.

As puddles appear, we leap with a cheer,
Jumping with gusto, not showing a fear.
We splash like two dolphins, oh what a sight,
A path that we carve, both silly and bright.

In this waltz we create, no time for a frown,
With each wacky step, in our topsy-turvy town.
Let's make some more memories, let's dance till we're done,
Side by side forever, we laugh and we run.

Bonded by the Ground We Cover

As we stroll hand in hand, the world feels so wide,
With our quirks and our giggles, it's one crazy ride.
With small leaps and bounds, we set off together,
Two silly explorers, through all kinds of weather.

The sidewalks our canvas, we paint with our feet,
Each stomp a new masterpiece, not missing a beat.
We shuffle and slide, in a quirky parade,
With each step a story, our laughter displayed.

Oh, the pot holes we dodge, oh the grass that we roam,
With mismatched directions, we're far from alone.
Like two peas in a pod, we wander and roam,
Stumbling through miles, this chaos feels home.

Through puddles and rainbows, our footprints will gleam,

In this silly ballet, we're living the dream.
Bonded by laughter, together we're free,
Every silly step tells a tale made for three.

The Rhythm of Our Stride

In the dance of our steps, we step on a beat,
Like a pair of clowns in a two-step repeat.
With every odd coziness, our laughter erupts,
Clumsy choreography, our joy truly jumps.

Like ducks on a pond, we waddle and sway,
The rhythm we find, makes perfection decay.
Footloose and fancy, we trip over air,
In this comical shuffle, without a care.

Every misstep a spark, lighting joy in our hearts,
Creating a melody as silliness starts.
From twirls to sways, we own the parade,
The rhythm of our friendship, pure magic displayed.

So here's to our journey, each stride a delight,
In giggles and grace, we dance through the night.
With every small stumble, let's give it a cheer,
For in this funny waltz, it's you that I hold dear.

Soles Across the Miles

With laces tangled, we embark,
Two feet lighter than a lark.
Each step a giggle, side by side,
In mismatched colors, we take pride.

We wander off on silly trails,
Where flip-flops flopped and nobody fails.
With every stomp, we leave our mark,
Dancing through puddles, making sparks.

A marathon of laughs and cheer,
We trade our socks, no need to fear.
In rubber boots or heels so bright,
Our journey shines, a pure delight.

From tiny toes to oversized clogs,
We skip through life, avoiding fogs.
With silly soles, we slide and glide,
Adventure awaits on this wild ride.

Navigation of Hearts

In sneakers' grip, we chart the seas,
With mapless hearts, we roam with ease.
A waltz through crosswalks, hand in hand,
We stumble on giggles, oh, isn't it grand?

We swipe left on serious strife,
Patting our soles, this is our life.
In each direction, laughter steers,
Hopping through puddles, chasing cheers.

With canvas dreams and shoelaced fates,
We dance through life's open gates.
A trek of jests and playful pranks,
We fill our backpacks with happy ranks.

Navigating through sneakered delights,
Our hearts compass, ready for sights.
In flip-flops or lace, we glide,
Banter flowing as our true guide.

Footwear of Union

In this collection of quirky pairs,
We unite in stripes, and colorful flares.
With boots that squeak and sandals that squeal,
Every step a chuckle, that's our deal.

When one gets lost in a giant heap,
We find old sandals that still make us leap.
With tongues that flop and backs that creak,
In this crazy dance, we never sneak.

From platforms high to flats that glide,
Every ground conquered with laughter wide.
In pre-loved shoes, our stories unfold,
Together we make memories gold.

So let's laugh through puddles, one trip, one shoe,
In this journey of fun, it's me and you.
With quirky pairs and hearts aligned,
Our footwear speaks, it's beautifully designed.

United Footsteps

With mismatched pairs and matching smiles,
We wander through life, across the miles.
In cropped pants or skirts swaying free,
Our journey shines, just you and me.

We step on toes, but never fret,
In each misstep, more joy begets.
With clumsy spins and unexpected falls,
We laugh off the stumbles, hear our calls.

From quirky heels to fuzzy socks,
Our feet do the talking, no need for locks.
Jumping in puddles, unleashing our cheer,
With every footfall, love draws near.

Through all the chaos, joy remains,
In each silly dance, no need for chains.
We leap, we frolic, our hearts take flight,
With united footsteps, all feels so right.

Trails of Togetherness

In mismatched clogs we skip along,
The echoes of laughter sing a song.
With every step, our feet collide,
As we tumble forth, side by side.

We trudge through puddles, splash and squish,
Making memories, an endless wish.
In flip-flops flying, oh, the grace,
Two clumsy souls in a silly race.

Around the corner, we trip and trip,
On roots and rocks, our friendship's grip.
With every stumble, winks exchanged,
We cherish chaos, perfectly arranged.

Together we wander, a joyful spree,
On this wild path, just you and me.
Our adventures wacky, nothing less,
In the dance of life, we're truly blessed.

Companions on the Trail

With squishy sandals and socks so bright,
We march like penguins, what a sight!
Through overgrown grass and patches of mud,
Lucky we are, not stuck in a flood!

Lost in giggles, we take the lead,
Chasing butterflies, planting a seed.
Every misstep a chance to roar,
Our feet create stories, never a bore.

Wobbly dancers on uneven ground,
We twirl and spin, never look around.
Laughter erupts as we tumble down,
Two silly pals with a grin, not a frown.

On this merry jaunt, we jaunt and hop,
Up hills and dales, we can't seem to stop.
With every blunder, a memory made,
In this joyful chaos, we'll never fade.

Paired Paths

Stride by stride, we find our pace,
With giggles bouncing all over the place.
Tangled up with our loops and knots,
We navigate life, whether it's hot or not.

In sneakers squeaking, we make our way,
Through fields of daisies, let's frolic and play.
With every misstep, a silly cheer,
Wherever we wander, we banish fear.

Clumsy shuffles on trails that twist,
Who'd thought walking could be such a quest?
With each little glitch, oh what a thrill,
Our laughter a melody, time seems to stand still.

As daylight dims and stars begin to peek,
We stroll through dreamscapes, our paths unique.
Two hearts encased in this playful dance,
In every side-step, an odd romance.

The Dance of Our Feet

With a jig and a jog, we prance about,
Feet all a-flutter, let's jump and shout!
In puddles we splash with a gleeful cheer,
Each leap a reminder that fun's always near.

We shuffle through leaves, with a crunch and a crack,
Our silly antics, no chance to hold back.
Two dancing fools lost in the beat,
Together we waltz on this whimsical street.

Side by side, we conquer the lanes,
In our own world, with giggles like trains.
Every stomp, every wiggle, a funny affair,
In this joyous rhythm, we lose all care.

So let's twirl and swirl right under the moon,
With steps so absurd, we'll finish too soon.
In this crazy dance of our wandering feet,
Life's muddled journey is wonderfully sweet.

Wanderlust

My soles are worn, they cry for fun,
Each step a giggle, under the sun.
Adventures beckon, where shall we roam?
With every stride, I'm never alone.

Bumping into puddles, leaping with glee,
Can you handle this wild spree?
With every tickle, and laughter near,
We'll dance through the chaos, never fear.

Together

In mismatched pairs, let's make a scene,
You in polka dots, me in marine.
Strutting like peacocks, such a sight,
Together we wander, day and night.

Through halls of laughter, we'll glide and sway,
Like silly mice on a ballet tray.
Our footprints tango, across the floor,
With every giggle, who could ask for more?

Treads of Trust

Side by side, through thick and thin,
You step first, I'll just dive in.
With every stomp, our bond grows strong,
In our own world, where we belong.

I'll follow you down the wobbly lane,
Counting the giggles, forgetting the pain.
Trust me, follow, and share the chase,
Together we make the wildest race.

The Art of Shared Movement

Two left feet, but who really cares?
We'll fumble and tumble without any fears.
In this dance of friendship, we take the chance,
Spinning in circles, lost in our trance.

Every shuffle's a laugh, every twirl's a scream,
Painting the sidewalk with our crazy dream.
In perfect harmony, we skip and twine,
No rhythm required, just yours and mine.

Echoing Steps

Listen closely, hear the sound,
Of echoing steps as we roll around.
Each stomp a signal, a playful beat,
Together we're nimble, we can't be beat.

As we prance across this leafy stage,
The world is our canvas, let's engage.
High-fives and laughter, our joyful quest,
In the symphony of fun, we are the best!

The Way We Travel

When I put on my left, you hop on the right,
Together we trip, but oh what a sight!
Flipping coins for the path, we giggle and cheer,
Every step feels like laughter, my friend, you are near.

You bring that odd sock, I'll wear a bright hat,
As we dance through the puddles and laugh at the splat!
We swing through the park, like kids in a play,
Inventing our journey, come what may.

Our feet might be big, but our joy is much more,
Each waddle and bob gets us through every door.
We'll navigate life with a map made of chuckles,
Adventure awaits, let's conquer those rumbles!

With each tiny step, we flip ordinary to grand,
Making memories as silly as we planned.
So here's to our strides, to every wild way,
Together we'll stumble, come join in our play.

Shared Trails

In mismatched zippers, we wander with flair,
Two pairs of mismatched fun, but we don't care!
Each step brings a giggle, each jaunt is a show,
With squeaky shoes bouncing, we're never too slow.

I'll step in your puddle, you'll hop over mine,
Not worried 'bout mud, we just laugh and we shine!
Our paths may be twisted like a pretzel in cheer,
But on this wild journey, the joys are so clear.

We'll take silly selfies and pose in the grass,
Two goofballs united, with a camera flash!
With hearts beating fast and our spirits so light,
Every trail that we share becomes pure delight.

So let's race the sunset and chase after the moon,
With laces all tangled, we sing our own tune.
On these shared little trails, we're never alone,
With laughter as fuel, we've both found our home.

The Comfort of Your Presence

With your comfy old sneakers and my crazy bright kicks,
We shuffle through life, sharing laughter and tricks.
Your toes peek a bit, while mine dance like flies,
Wobbly companions, under deepening skies.

When our feet say 'ouch', and we laugh through the pain,
We make up new dances like 'The Shuffle of Rain'.
With each funny fall, we just giggle and sit,
Sharing stories of how we both stumbled a bit.

Our mismatched rhythms make a beat so divine,
With every small step, we're still doing just fine.
In the comfort of chaos, where hearts can collide,
Nothing feels better than having you by my side.

Let's twirl through the air, like goofballs afloat,
In sneakers of giggles, on this wild little boat.
We may trip, we may tumble, but that's how it goes,
For in every misstep, our friendship just grows.

Together We Wander

We're two wandering souls, with a flair for the mix,
With steps set to laughter and hearts full of tricks.
Every misstep leads us to giggles galore,
As we badger the flowers, and dance by the shore.

In flip-flops or clogs, we stride with great style,
Jumps that could rival a circus for a while.
We'll wear crazy outfits, with colors so loud,
In our whimsical journey, forever we're proud.

With each little trip, we make magic anew,
Inventing our sorrows, painting skies bright and blue.
Together we wander, our joy like confetti,
In the great parade of life, we keep it all ready.

So let's dance with the stars and play in the sun,
Two pals on a mission, now that's really fun!
Hand in hand, let's go, where the path takes us true,
Forever in laughter, it's just me and you.

The Embrace of Steps

In mismatched kicks, we prance with flair,
Our feet like comedians, dancing in air.
One's too big, the other's just right,
Step by step, we giggle with delight.

Each misstep echoes with joyous sound,
A waltz of awkwardness, twirling around.
Together we stumble, but never we fall,
In this grand adventure, we're having a ball.

With squeaky soles and laces untied,
We're a circus of laughter, so silly with pride.
Every step's a joke, every mile's a jest,
In our playful journey, we are truly blessed.

Through puddles and paths, our shenanigans flow,
Each toe-tapping scene is a fantastic show.
In footwear of whimsy, we wander and sway,
Together we shine, come what may.

Journeys Interwoven

In quirky attire, we navigate roads,
With clashing colors, like comic book codes.
Your left foot's a giant, my right's quite a clown,
Yet laughter unites us as we step up and down.

We dance on the pavement, a whimsical pair,
Each giggle a footprint, a tale we can share.
Uneven adventures, with bumps in the street,
But every misstep turns sour into sweet.

Our soles tell a story of love and of fun,
In mismatched mischief, we shine like the sun.
With each playful scuffle, we create a groove,
In this waltz of the weird, we always improve.

Together we wander, what a wild ride!
With every footpath, our hearts open wide.
Each step is a chuckle, every mile a song,
In this quirky journey, we always belong.

Footfalls of Affection

With hoots and hollers, we strut through the park,
Our shoes are as loud as a Broadway spark.
You trip on your laces, I trip on my charm,
Together we fumble, but it's always warm.

Each footfall's a giggle, a tickle of cheer,
In patterned socks, we chase away fear.
With every stumble, our laughter resounds,
In the theater of life, we dance all around.

We kick up the dust with our silly parade,
Our footprints are wild, like a grand charade.
Through fields of green and the streets oh so gray,
We leap over puddles, come what may.

With shoes full of stories, we cherish the day,
In the world of the whimsical, we've found our way.
On this path of affection, where fun never ends,
Together we wander, as the best of friends.

Together on the Trail

With floppy old sandals, we tackle the lane,
My left foot's a rebel, your right drives me insane.
We giggle at squirrels, who laugh as we pass,
Our antics and laughter as light as the grass.

In boots made for dancing and sneakers of flair,
We skip through the breezes, without a care.
Each step's a reminder of joys that we've found,
In this merry romp, where friendship abounds.

Tiny blisters and scrapes become tales that we tell,
As we rally together, we laugh through each fell.
In this whirlwind of footfalls, we dance 'til the night,
With the moon as our spotlight, everything feels right.

We shuffle and play, our spirits so spry,
Two goofy explorers beneath a vast sky.
In our parade of peculiar, we always delight,
Together on the trail, our hearts take flight.

www.ingramcontent.com/pod-product-compliance
Lightning Source LLC
Chambersburg PA
CBHW050305120526
44590CB00016B/2499